THE HIDDEN RULES OF CATS

How Tiny Shifts in You Transform the Bond You Share

Copyright © 2025

All rights reserved. No portion of this book, including but not limited to text, images, or any other content, may be reproduced, distributed, transmitted, or stored in any form or by any means, whether electronic, mechanical, photocopying, recording, or by any other information storage and retrieval system, without prior written permission from the author. This includes any form of publication, online or offline, in whole or in part, or in any derivative work, whether now known or hereafter invented. Unauthorized use of any material from this book is prohibited and may result in legal action.

Table of Contents

Introduction 4

Chapter 1: Understanding Your Cat's Mind 7

Chapter 2: Preparing Your Home for Training Success 12

Chapter 3: Litter Box Training – Fast & Fuss-Free 18

Chapter 4: Stopping Scratching Without Punishment 23

Chapter 5: Yes, You Can Teach Cats Commands 28

Chapter 6: Solving the 5 Most Common Cat Problems 33

Chapter 7: The Power of Play-Based Training 39

Chapter 8: Cat Training Myths That Hold You Back 44

Chapter 9: Bonus Training – Leash, Travel, and Vet Visits 49

Chapter 10: Your First 30 Days – A Simple Training Plan 54

Introduction

Featuring Emily & Miso

When Emily adopted Miso, she expected a cozy lap cat. What she got instead was a mystery wrapped in fur. One moment he was purring; the next, he was biting the air like he was settling a score.

On day two, he tore across the living room, scaled her curtains, knocked over her coffee, and calmly sat on her laptop. As Emily stared at the chaos, Miso blinked slowly, as if to say, *Welcome to cat ownership, rookie.*

But Emily didn't give up. She adjusted. She paid attention. In time, so did Miso.

What started as confusion became connection, not through control, but through understanding. Emily didn't try to make Miso obedient. She simply learned to speak his language. And he responded.

Why This Book Exists

This guide isn't about turning your cat into a circus act. It's about building communication, trust, and habits that work for both of you.

It's for:

- New cat parents (especially of rescues or rehomes)
- Those considering whether a cat is right for them
- Anyone who's ever said, "I love my cat...but I don't *get* him."

INTRODUCTION

You'll learn how to:

- Read your cat's behavior and body language
- Set up your home for training success
- Solve common issues without punishment
- Teach useful commands and routines
- Build a bond that lasts

No, you don't need to be perfect. You just need to be patient.

ONE CAT, ONE MONTH, ONE JOURNEY

This book follows one month in the life of Emily and Miso—a first-time cat owner and her unpredictable companion. You'll see what real-life cat training looks like: the good, the weird, and the surprisingly rewarding.

Whether your cat is cuddly, cautious, or borderline unhinged, this guide will help you build a calm, curious, and cooperative relationship.

Let's get started.

Chapter 1: Understanding Your Cat's Mind

CHAPTER 1: UNDERSTANDING YOUR CAT'S MIND

OPENING STORY: "THE GREAT COUCH STAKEOUT"

Emily thought she was ready. She had the treats, the cozy fleece bed, and even a monogrammed food bowl that said "Miso" in tasteful gold script. A friend had joked, "You've basically adopted a prince," and she'd laughed—because that's exactly what it felt like.

But once Miso arrived, all royal pretense vanished. He bolted under the couch the moment she set down the carrier. Not a graceful glide but an outright panic sprint. She didn't even know he could move that fast.

"Okay, cool," she whispered, kneeling. "You're just getting your bearings. Totally normal."

Day one passed. So did day two. He emerged once at 3:12 a.m., stared at her as if *she* were the intruder, and vanished again.

Emily lay flat on the living room floor by day three, talking into the dust bunnies. "Do you hate me? I bought you organic food. I vacuumed."

A faint rustle came from under the couch. Miso's eye blinked at her. Then: nothing.

She didn't know it then, but he wasn't mad. He wasn't plotting. He was doing what cats do—watching, listening, and deciding.

Looking back, she would laugh at how quickly she'd panicked. But at the time? She Googled "my cat hates me" more times than she'd care to admit.

What's Really Going On?

Cats don't rush into friendships. They don't fetch because it makes you happy, and they definitely don't love new environments on day one.

Miso wasn't being cold. He was being *careful*. Cats are solo survivors by nature. In the wild, caution kept them alive. In your home, it just looks like distance.

What Emily didn't realize (and honestly, who does at first?) was that Miso's silence wasn't a sign of dislike; it was a sign he was processing. Watching. Calculating: **"Is this safe? Is this mine? Can I leave if I need to?"**

How Cats Learn: Instinct + Experience

Your cat's behavior isn't random. Two things shape it:

- **Instinct** – hiding, scratching, chasing, and watching from afar.
- **Experience** – learning what happens after they try something.

Emily learned this one breakfast at a time.

If she fed Miso, then made a loud noise (like dropping the coffee scoop), he'd vanish. If she crouched quietly and offered a treat with an outstretched hand, he'd consider it.

Over time, patterns formed. He learned *she* wasn't a threat. She learned *he* needed space.

CHAPTER 1: UNDERSTANDING YOUR CAT'S MIND

Training Starts with Trust

Before training a cat, you need to capture their attention. Before that, you need their trust.

Here's what finally worked for Emily:

- Sitting on the floor and ignoring him (painful for extroverts)
- Feeding at consistent times
- Avoiding any fast, unpredictable movements like opening a chip bag too close to him.

Trust isn't instant; rather, it builds slowly—one quiet moment at a time.

> **Emily's Mini-Moment: "The Slow Blink Breakthrough"**

Two weeks in, Miso still startled when she walked too fast. He tolerated her, but "companionship" wasn't exactly the word.

Then one night, Emily sat cross-legged on the floor, exhausted from another day of trying. She looked over at Miso, who had settled five feet away like a tiny security guard.

She blinked. Slowly. No expectation.

And miracle of miracles, he blinked back.

She didn't cry. (Okay, maybe one tear. A small one.)

That night, he stayed in the room when she stood up. The next day, he sniffed her hand without bolting.

It wasn't dramatic. It wasn't a movie moment. But it was theirs.

Decoding Cat Communication

Cats don't talk, but they're always communicating. Emily became fluent in the basics:

- **Ears forward** = curious
- **Tail twitching** = annoyed
- **Puffed tail** = do not proceed
- **Half-closed eyes** = all is well
- **Direct stare** = maybe love…maybe judgment

The biggest lesson? If a cat's tail is wagging like a dog's…you're in danger.

> **Key Takeaways (With a Few Human Truths)**
> - Your cat isn't broken if they hide. You're not failing if they don't cuddle.
> - Behavior is communication. "Why is he doing this?" becomes "What is he telling me?"
> - Patience isn't just a virtue; it's the foundation of every step you'll take from here.

Chapter 2: Preparing Your Home for Training Success

Opening Story: "Miso's Grand Tour"

By the time Miso appeared from under the couch, Emily thought the hard part was over.

Spoiler: it wasn't.

He didn't stroll out with gratitude or curiosity. He crept, slow and silent, inspecting every corner like a cat detective in a murder mystery. He sniffed the food bowl. Ignored it. Sniffed the litter box. Turned his back. Walked past the cactus-shaped scratcher like it was beneath him.

Then, without a sound, he leapt onto the bookshelf, batted a ceramic owl to its death, and perched like he owned the place.

Emily stared at the owl. Then at Miso.

"This is fine," she said aloud, because that's what you say when things aren't.

Looking back, Emily realized she'd prepared her home for *her* idea of a cat, not for the actual one currently conquering her furniture.

Your Home, According to a Cat

To you, your apartment is a space with a style. To your cat, it's uncharted wilderness. Emily saw a cozy studio. Miso saw:

- No guaranteed exits
- Loud appliances that could be monsters

- Flat surfaces begging to be climbed
- Absolutely nowhere to hide except under the sofa.

Cats don't care about your design aesthetic. They care about:

- Where can they run
- Where they can watch you
- Where they won't be ambushed by a vacuum

How Emily Adapted (After a Few Failures)

Some changes happened fast. Others...not so much.

Here's what worked (eventually):

1. A Place to Disappear in Peace

Emily had proudly set up Miso's "cat corner" in the living room: plush bed, window view, even a motivational sign that said, "Purr More, Hiss Less." Miso ignored it entirely.

What he did like was a cardboard box in the closet with an old hoodie inside.

Lesson: Cats don't need luxury. They need safety.

2. The Litter Box Location Fail

Emily put the litter box next to the washing machine. Out of sight, convenient for cleaning, and very logical.

Miso used her bathmat instead.

After some Googling, she relocated the box to a quieter spot and replaced the scented litter with unscented.

Miso used it within the hour. She almost cried.

Checklist:
- One box per cat
- Quiet, accessible location
- Unscented, clumping litter
- Scoop daily. Yes, daily.

3. Scratching Preferences (and Aesthetic Regrets)

Emily bought a cactus-shaped scratcher. Instagram loved it. Miso didn't.

The plain sisal-wrapped post she got on sale and shoved in the corner is what he preferred. Once she moved it next to his nap spot, he adopted it as if it were made of gold.

4. Vertical Territory is Non-Negotiable

Miso was not content to live horizontally. The bookshelf was tempting. The kitchen counter? Too tempting.

Emily finally gave in and bought a cat tree. Within thirty seconds, Miso was perched at the top, tail swishing in triumph.

▌Emily's Mini-Moment: "The 8 p.m. Play Alarm"

She didn't *mean* to create a routine. She just had time around 8 p.m. and played with Miso while half-watching a baking show.

By the third night, he was waiting by the toy closet at 7:58 p.m.

If she was late, he meowed. If she was *really* late, he started batting the closet door like a drum.

Lesson: If you don't make a routine, your cat will.

ROUTINE = STABILITY (FOR BOTH OF YOU)

Once Emily added structured feeding times, play sessions, and wind-down time, everything got easier. Miso stopped hiding. Stopped nighttime zoomies (mostly). Started sitting by the kitchen right before dinner like a tiny, punctual roommate.

Try this sample rhythm:

- Morning: Feed + short play
- Afternoon: Solo nap or window patrol
- Evening: Wand toy session + training + meal
- Night: Calm bonding—brushing, petting, maybe a shared podcast (Emily's idea, not Miso's)

WHAT DIDN'T WORK (BUT MIGHT SOUND FAMILIAR)

- Scented litter: smelled like lavender to Emily, but to Miso, it smelled like danger.

- Tucking the scratcher behind the dryer: out of sight, out of use.
- Buying everything at once: Miso was overwhelmed. He glared at the new items like they were suspicious intruders.

Final Takeaways

- Set up your space for your *actual* cat, not your Pinterest board.
- Focus on safety, height, and routine—your cat will thank you with fewer "gifts" in inconvenient places.
- Don't rush. A calm, functional setup beats fancy gear every time.
- Your cat doesn't want perfection. They want a place that makes sense—on *their* terms.

Chapter 3: Litter Box Training - Fast & Fuss-Free

Opening Story: "The Case of the Dining Room Deposit"

Emily had read the blogs. She'd followed the setup checklist. Clean litter box? Check. Tucked in a quiet-ish corner of the laundry room? Check. With a little privacy flap? Check again.

So, when she found a suspicious deposit under her dining table, she was confused. Horrified. Mildly betrayed.

"I gave you the deluxe setup," she whispered to the stain on the rug. "Why would you choose the floor?"

Miso didn't answer. He was too busy batting a bread twist-tie under the couch.

At first, she assumed he was being defiant. It took a few frustrating days (and several deep-cleaning sessions) before she realized the truth: the laundry room sounded like a jet engine, smelled like fabric softener, and to a nervous cat, it might as well have been a trap.

Why Cats Avoid the Box (Even When It's Right There)

The good news? Most cats are instinctively drawn to using litter. It satisfies their natural "bury and go" instinct.

The bad news is that if they're *not* using it, something's wrong, and it's your job to play detective.

Common reasons cats boycott the box:

- The location is loud, exposed, or hard to access
- The litter is scented or recently changed
- The box is too small, too deep, or covered (some cats hate enclosed spaces)
- It isn't cleaned often enough
- There's an underlying medical issue

If your cat stops using the box, don't assume it's a behavioral issue. Rule out pain or discomfort first. Emily didn't have to make a vet trip, but she did move the box. That was all it took.

What Really Works

Once Emily adjusted the setup, the problem vanished. No stern lectures or sprays. Just a quieter corner and a different kind of litter.

Here's what made the difference:

- **Box type:** Open, large, and easy to escape from
- **Litter:** Unscented, clumping
- **Location:** Quiet bathroom instead of laundry room
- **Routine:** Scooped every day, full refresh weekly

The transformation was almost immediate. Miso went from avoiding the box to using it like a seasoned pro.

> **Emily's Mini-Moment: "The Five-Dollar Box Upgrade"**

"Once I made the switch, things improved," Emily said—but not perfectly. Two days later, Miso surprised her with a very pointed protest poop behind the bathroom door.

Emily sighed. "Okay, still negotiating."

She added another box in a second quiet location. That one? Instant hit. Apparently, Miso wanted options.

Lesson: Sometimes cats need more than just "the right spot." They want choices, too.

KITTENS VS. ADULTS: DIFFERENT STARTING POINTS

For kittens:

- Guide them to the box after meals, naps, or play
- Reward success with praise or a treat
- Stay calm, accidents happen

For adult cats or rescues:

- Start in a small space (one room) with easy access to the box
- Expand their territory gradually
- Watch for signs of aversion (like scratching near the box but not in it)

Emily also learned that even background noise like the hum of a nearby fan could throw Miso off.

When Accidents Happen (Because They Will)

Take a breath. Clean up. Move on.

Cats don't understand punishment, but they *do* remember environments that felt unsafe, rushed, or just plain unpleasant.

Cleanup tips that work:

- Use enzymatic cleaners to erase scent trails
- Avoid bleach or vinegar, as some cats find them attractive
- Temporarily block off accident zones—or place food there (cats rarely eliminate near meals)

Key Takeaways (No Shame Required)

- A cat avoiding the box isn't being rebellious; they're making a judgment call.
- Prioritize comfort, quiet, and cleanliness over convenience.
- Don't assume "fancy" means "functional." Your cat will let you know what works for them.
- Trust is built in the little things, including where they choose to go.

Chapter 4: Stopping Scratching Without Punishment

CHAPTER 4: STOPPING SCRATCHING WITHOUT PUNISHMENT

OPENING STORY: "THE COUCH THAT FOUGHT BACK"

The first time Emily heard it, she didn't even know what it was.

SCRITCH-SCRITCH-SCRITCH.

She turned slowly, coffee mid-sip, to find Miso with both paws buried in the arm of her brand-new couch, his claws working a steady rhythm like he was performing surgery.

"Miso!" she blurted. He looked up, mildly surprised, and then bolted behind the bookshelf like a little gray outlaw.

She tried everything over the next week: citrus sprays, sticky tape, even a roll of foil. Miso was briefly confused and then resumed his work on the opposite side of the couch.

By the end of the week, the sofa was wearing more protective tape than actual upholstery.

WHY CATS SCRATCH (AND WHY YOU CAN'T STOP IT)

Here's the thing: cats scratch. Not because they're defiant, not because they're trying to destroy your stuff, but because they *need* to.

Scratching is essential. It helps them:

- Stretch their bodies
- Sharpen and shed old claw sheaths

- Mark territory (both visually and with scent glands in their paws)
- Relieve stress or excitement

Trying to "stop" scratching altogether is like trying to stop a toddler from making noise. It's not going to happen. The better approach is to *redirect* it to something that makes sense to both of you.

Emily's Learning Curve

At first, Emily assumed Miso was "acting out." But once she realized scratching was non-negotiable, she shifted her strategy. Instead of asking *"How do I stop this?"*, she asked *"What would he rather scratch?"*

She bought a tall sisal-wrapped post and placed it next to the couch.

Miso ignored it for three days.

Then, during a mid-afternoon zoomie, he paused by the post, gave it one experimental swipe, and kept going.

That night, Emily rubbed a little catnip into the rope. The next morning, she woke to the sound of—yes—**scritch-scritch-scritch.** But this time, it was the post.

Progress.

What Actually Worked

Emily didn't have a system at first. But over time, she pieced together what helped:

- **Scratchers in key spots** near the couch, by the window, and beside his nap zone.
- **Different types:** one vertical, another flat.
- **Praise**—every time he used it, he got a "Good boy" and sometimes a treat.

After a few weeks, Miso's couch attacks stopped. Not because he "learned his lesson," but because he finally had a better choice.

Emily's Mini-Moment: "The Wrong Scratchers"

Emily originally bought a trendy cardboard scratcher shaped like a cactus. It looked amazing in photos.

Miso hated it.

He preferred the cheap vertical post that didn't match anything in the apartment. But he used it daily.

Lesson: Appeal to your cat's *texture* preferences, not your *Instagram* feed.

CONSISTENCY OVER CORRECTION

Every time Emily scolded Miso for scratching the couch, he'd wait until she wasn't looking. However, when she redirected him by moving the scratcher closer and rewarding him when he used it, he started choosing it on his own.

She didn't need to yell. She just needed to make the right choice *easier* than the wrong one.

What Emily Stopped Doing (Eventually)

- **Yelling "No!"** – It startled him, sure. But it didn't teach him anything.
- **Using water spray** – She tried it once. He disappeared for hours. That was enough.
- **Declawing?** – Never. Not even considered. (Emily had read enough to know it's painful, irreversible, and closer to amputation than grooming.)

Final Thoughts

Scratching isn't a battle—it's a conversation.

If your cat is scratching something you hate, the message isn't "I'm evil." It's "I need to stretch, de-stress, or mark my space—and this is the best thing I've got."

The solution isn't punishment. It's redirection, reward, and smart furniture placement.

And maybe, if you're lucky, a scratcher your cat truly likes.

Chapter 5: Yes, You Can Teach Cats Commands

Opening Story: "Come... On, Please?"

Emily stood in the hallway, shaking the treat bag as if summoning spirits. "Miso, come here!" she called, for the third time.

No response.

She peeked into the living room. Miso was perched atop the bookshelf, staring right at her. His eyes said, *"I hear you. I've simply weighed the options."*

Emily sighed. "You're smart. Why won't you act like it?"

She wasn't wrong. Miso *was* smart. What she didn't realize yet was that he needed a reason, not just a command.

Yes, Cats Can Be Trained. But It's a Negotiation.

If you've ever been told cats are untrainable, that's a myth.

They can absolutely learn commands—but they're not wired to follow orders. They're solo decision-makers. They do things because those things pay off.

Training a cat isn't about dominance. It's about clarity, consistency, and, yes, excellent bribes.

Training Is a Pattern, Not a Power Move

Emily didn't sit Miso down and give him a lecture. She just started dropping treats.

Literally.

She'd say "come" and toss a treat near her feet. At first, Miso ignored it. Then he noticed and walked over. By day three, he was already halfway to her the moment he heard the word.

No clicker yet. No structured sessions. Just repeated associations.

Useful Commands That Matter

Some cat tricks are for fun. But a few are surprisingly practical:

- **Come** – Redirect mischief, call them in from hiding, or just bond.
- **Sit** – Handy during feeding, grooming, or when greeting guests.
- **High Five** – Fun, impressive, and boosts confidence.
- **Stay / Wait** – Useful at doors or in crates.
- **Off** – For keeping counters cat-free (or at least cat-less when you're looking).

Emily found that starting with "come" built the foundation. Once Miso got the hang of it, other commands came more easily.

Well...sometimes.

Emily's Mini-Moment: "The Accidental Sit"

Emily didn't even realize she was training "sit." She just happened to say it every time she reached for the treat drawer.

One day, Miso sat down automatically. She blinked.

"Oh. That's...okay then."

Lesson: Even casual routines can become training, whether you mean to or not.

Tools That Help (But Aren't Required)

Emily didn't use a clicker at first, but when she did, Miso seemed to catch on faster. He liked knowing *exactly* when he'd done the right thing.

Here's what helped:

- Small, soft treats that didn't take forever to chew.
- A quiet room (the blender was a training killer).
- 3-5 minute sessions max, cats don't do marathons.
- A consistent marker: Emily said "Yes!" instead of using a clicker at first.

When It Doesn't Work Right Away

There were plenty of days when Miso just...didn't.

He'd walk halfway toward Emily, stop, and sit facing the opposite direction. He once jumped *over* the treat she'd just tossed. He occasionally pretended he didn't know what "come" meant if there wasn't a bribe involved.

Emily learned not to take it personally. Some days are just *cat days*.

She also learned to **stop** training while it was still fun for both of them. Overdoing it only led to eye squints and slow tail flicks.

Simple Training Framework (No Charts Required)

1. **Cue** – Use a clear word, such as "come" or "sit".
2. **Action** – Lure with a treat or gesture.
3. **Mark** – Click or say "yes!" the moment it happens.
4. **Reward** – Give the treat immediately.

That's it. No buzzers. No flashcards. Just clarity and consistency.

Final Takeaways

- **Cats *can* be trained**, but they expect something in return.
- **Start small** and keep it fun. You're building communication.
- **Your cat is learning even when you're not trying to teach.**
- **Progress isn't linear. That's okay. You're raising a roommate, not programming a robot.**

Chapter 6: Solving the 5 Most Common Cat Problems

CHAPTER 6: SOLVING THE 5 MOST COMMON CAT PROBLEMS

Opening Story: "The 3 a.m. Stampede"

Emily had just drifted off to sleep, dreaming of a version of Miso that liked naps and bookshelves more than chaos.

Then—*SKRRRTCH-thump-thump-thump—CRASH.*

She bolted upright.

There he was. Miso. Racing down the hallway like his tail was on fire. He rebounded off the couch arm, vaulted onto the table, and launched himself into the curtains with the elegance of a drunken squirrel.

It was 3:12 a.m.

Emily rubbed her face and muttered, "What *is* wrong with you?"

Miso paused mid-zoom, blinked slowly, and trotted off. Mission complete.

First, Let's Redefine "Bad Behavior"

Most cat "problems" aren't about defiance. They're about biology, unmet needs, or a cat trying to communicate in a language we haven't learned yet.

If your cat bites, scratches, bolts, chews, or sprints like they're auditioning for a wildlife documentary, it's not to spite you. It's because something in their environment or routine isn't quite right.

Emily didn't solve these things with rules. She solved them with patience, observation, and a lot of trial and error.

Let's examine the five most common issues and how they played out with Miso.

1. Nighttime Zoomies

(a.k.a. The 3 a.m. Olympics)

Cats are crepuscular. That means they're wired to be most active around dawn and dusk. Which is adorable when they gently stretch at sunrise—and *less* cute when they barrel down the hallway like a bowling ball at midnight.

What helped:

- A ten-minute wand toy session around 8 p.m.
- Feeding right after to simulate "hunt, eat, sleep."
- Keeping the house dark and quiet after nine.

Within a week, Miso shifted his "race time" to 7 p.m. And by 10, he was passed out like a stuffed animal.

2. Biting and Rough Play

Miso loved attention. He also loved pouncing on Emily's ankles when she walked by. Cute when he was a kitten—less cute with adult teeth involved.

She realized a bit too late that she had accidentally taught him hands were toys. During early play sessions, she'd wiggled her fingers. He remembered.

What helped:

- Using only toys during play—no fingers or feet.
- Withdrawing attention instantly if he bit.
- Redirecting to a toy and praising gentle play.

It took time. And a few sock casualties. But Miso learned: gentle = play continues. Teeth = play stops.

3. Overstimulation Swats

(*a.k.a. "Pet Me—Okay That's Enough—TOO MUCH"*)

Miso would be purring one moment, swatting the next. It confused Emily until she noticed the signals: tail twitching, ears turning sideways, and body stiffening.

He wasn't mad. He was overstimulated.

> **Emily's fix? She stopped pushing. Literally.**

She learned to end petting sessions *before* the tail twitch. She gave him breaks. She began using treats and toys to gradually build tolerance, especially for grooming and veterinary preparation.

Over time, Miso stopped swatting and started walking away when he'd had enough—a fair trade.

4. Jumping on Counters

Emily once walked into the kitchen to find Miso sitting in the sink, as if he were waiting for his espresso.

He wasn't trying to be bad. He was being a cat: curious, height-seeking, and deeply interested in the smells up there.

The fix was "No!" and "Yes, but over here."

- She got a tall cat tree and placed it near the kitchen.
- She rewarded him for choosing it over the counter.

Eventually, he learned that one gets him praise, while the other gets him ignored.

5. Destructive Chewing or Overgrooming

One week, Emily noticed Miso obsessively licking his leg and chewing the corner of the rug. The vet cleared him medically. The diagnosis? Boredom and stress.

It wasn't enough to *stop* the behavior—she had to *replace* it with something better.

What helped:

- New toys and puzzle feeders
- More play sessions, especially on solo days
- A window perch to give him something to watch

Once his brain and body were more engaged, the licking stopped. The rug survived.

Final Thoughts

Cat problems are rarely solved in a day. They're solved in dozens of tiny moments—noticing a tail twitch, trying something new when the last thing didn't work.

Emily didn't "fix" Miso. She worked with him, adjusted routines, and let some things go.

They didn't end up with a perfect pet-human relationship. They ended up with a **real one.**

Chapter 7: The Power of Play-Based Training

CHAPTER 7: THE POWER OF PLAY-BASED TRAINING

Opening Story: "The Wand That Saved the Blinds"

By week three, Emily was ready to admit defeat in one particular battle: the blinds.

Every afternoon while she worked, Miso launched himself into them with the grace of a demolition expert. Scolding didn't help. Rearranging the furniture didn't help. She even considered taking them down altogether and embracing a "no privacy" lifestyle.

Then, one night while digging through a drawer, she found a forgotten feather wand toy. Still in the packaging.

Out of options, she flicked it once across the living room floor.

Miso froze. His tail twitched. His pupils widened. The blinds were instantly irrelevant.

What followed was a fifteen-minute whirlwind of pounces, somersaults, and full-body flips. Miso collapsed on his side, panting and blissful.

The blinds? Untouched for the next two days.

Play Isn't Optional—It's Instinct

To a cat, play isn't entertainment—it's instinctual behavior. Hunting, chasing, stalking, pouncing: these are not "games" to your cat. They're survival patterns.

When you don't give an indoor cat a proper outlet for those patterns, they'll invent one—often involving your furniture.

Emily thought Miso was acting out. In reality, he doesn't play enough.

Play is Where Training Happens (Whether You Mean To or Not)

Once Emily made play part of her daily rhythm, she realized something surprising: it wasn't just reducing Miso's chaos. It was making training easier.

When he was already in "hunt" mode, he became more alert, more responsive, and more willing to engage with commands like "come" or "sit."

It wasn't obedience, exactly. It was *timing*. She wasn't trying to teach him during nap time or when he was in a food coma. She was meeting him where his brain already was: curious, focused, and ready to chase.

Emily's Experiment: Training Mid-Pounce

She started small. She'd flick the wand toy, then call, "Miso, come!" as he chased it.

He came. Not for the command but because she'd tied the word to movement and fun.

Eventually, she no longer needed the toy every time. The association stuck. It became a real cue.

Same with "sit." During a lull in play, she'd hold up a treat, say the word, and wait. His little butt hit the floor. She clicked, praised, and rewarded.

It didn't feel like training. It felt like playing smarter.

CHAPTER 7: THE POWER OF PLAY-BASED TRAINING

What Toys Work Well

Miso wasn't interested in things that didn't move. Balls that stayed still. Boring. Mice that didn't squeak. Ignored.

But:

- **Feather wands** were a hit.
- **Laser pointers** worked when followed by a "catchable" toy at the end.
- **Puzzle feeders** kept him engaged for long stretches.
- **Crinkle tunnels** gave him a mix of hiding, sprinting, and lurking.
- **Catnip toys?** Mood dependent. Some days, he was obsessed. Other days, completely unimpressed.

Emily kept a basket and rotated the options weekly. Variety turned out to be part of the magic.

Creating a Play Routine (Without Overthinking It)

The routine didn't come from a planner; it came from desperation.

Emily started playing with Miso around 8 p.m. simply because it fit into her schedule. By the third evening, he was already sitting by the toy drawer at 7:55, waiting like it was his job.

That consistency had a bonus: Miso was calmer at night. No more attacks on the blinds. No more midnight races. He played, ate, and slept—just like nature intended.

When Play Backfires (Yes, It Happens)

One night, Emily pushed the wand session a little too long. Miso went from excited to overstimulated. The tail flicking started. Then the batting. Then the growling.

She backed off, but it was a good reminder: **play is powerful, but so is knowing when to stop.**

Final Takeaways

- Play isn't a treat—it's a necessity for a healthy cat
- The right toy can solve many behavioral problems
- You can sneak training into play without structure or struggle
- Overstimulation is real—know when to wrap it up
- Consistency turns chaos into connection

Chapter 8: Cat Training Myths That Hold You Back

Opening Story: "Wait... You Trained Your Cat?"

Emily's friend Kelly came over one Saturday afternoon and barely had time to kick off her shoes before doing a double-take.

Miso was sitting calmly at the kitchen entrance, tail tucked neatly, looking like a tiny doorman.

"Wait," Kelly said. "Did...did you *train* your cat to sit?"

Emily smiled and casually tossed Miso a treat. "Sort of."

"He comes when you call, too," she added, walking to the fridge. "On a good day."

Kelly laughed. "You must've gotten one of those weird cats. Mine just stares at me like I owe him rent."

Emily didn't argue, but the thought lingered: *It's not that Miso is weird. It's that I stopped believing the myths.*

Myth #1: "Cats Can't Be Trained"

This is the myth that stops most people before they ever start. Cats *can* be trained, they're just not dogs.

Dogs follow leaders. Cats follow incentives.

If "sit" means a treat appears out of nowhere? They'll sit.

If "come" means playtime, dinner, or chin rubs? They'll eventually come (unless they're busy sitting just out of reach, watching you struggle).

Emily didn't train Miso by demanding compliance. She trained him by making it *worth his while*.

Myth #2: "Punishment Works"

Emily had tried yelling "No!" when Miso jumped on the counter.

She tried a squirt bottle. The betrayal in his eyes stuck with her longer than the behavior did.

Eventually, she realized punishment didn't stop the action. It just made Miso anxious around *her*.

When she switched to redirection and reward, praising him for climbing his cat tree instead of the sink, he started doing it. Because it felt good, not because he was afraid.

What *Does* Work

- **Redirection** – Give them something better to do.
- **Reinforcement** – Reward the behavior you want to see.
- **Routine** – Make good behavior predictable and easy.

Cats don't do guilt. They do logic.

Myth #3: "Only Kittens Can Learn"

Kittens may soak up new experiences like sponges, but adult and senior cats can learn just as well.

Miso was five months old when Emily brought him home, already opinionated and skeptical. Still, he picked up "come," "sit," and even "high five" within a few weeks.

Later, Emily helped her friend's cat, an eleven-year-old tabby named Tofu, learn to walk in a harness for daily courtyard strolls.

Age isn't a training barrier; it's a pacing adjustment.

Myth #4: "Training Makes Cats Less… Cat"

This one caught Emily off guard. At first, she worried that training might make Miso more obedient, sure—but also less *Miso*.

Instead, he became more confident. More expressive. He started offering behaviors—sitting unprompted, high-fiving visitors, walking into the carrier without a fuss.

Training didn't flatten his personality. It brought it into sharper focus.

Conversations Emily Didn't Expect to Have:

Kelly: "Why is your cat pawing at the air like he wants something?"

Emily: "He's asking for a treat."

Kelly: "I thought cats didn't do that."

Emily: "They do. If you listen."

Chapter 8: Cat Training Myths That Hold You Back

Final Takeaways

- Cats are *absolutely* trainable, but you need the right motivation to succeed.
- Punishment causes fear. Rewards build trust.
- Adult and senior cats can learn just as well as kittens.
- Training doesn't change who your cat is; it reveals who they've always been.

Chapter 9:
Bonus Training – Leash, Travel, and Vet Visits

CHAPTER 9: BONUS TRAINING – LEASH, TRAVEL, AND VET VISITS

Opening Story: "The Carrier of Doom"

The moment Emily pulled the carrier out of the closet, Miso vanished. One second he was sunbathing on the rug, the next gone. Not under the bed. Not in the closet. Somehow... inside the couch?

Twenty minutes, three treats, and one pulled shoulder later, Emily managed to coax him out and into the carrier.

The car ride was pure protest: yowling, pacing, a dramatic flop that suggested betrayal on a Shakespearean level.

By the time they arrived at the vet, they both looked as though they needed a sedative.

That night, Emily made a promise. "Next time, we *train* for this."

Why Bother Training for Travel and Vet Visits?

You may think: leash walking? Carrier training? For a cat?

But here's the truth: training for these "extras" makes everything else easier. Not just emergencies or appointments, but your relationship.

Less stress. More trust. And, yes, less drama in the wee hours when you need to stuff your cat into a box and get to an emergency vet.

Leash Training: The Great Outdoors (Kinda)

Miso loved the balcony. He'd press his face to the glass like he was watching a world he didn't belong to.

So, Emily wondered: *What if we opened that world up—just a little?*

She started slow. Letting him sniff the harness. Tossing treats inside it. The first time she clipped it on, he flopped like his spine had turned into overcooked pasta. But a few minutes and a little praise later, he stood up and walked around as if it were a fashion statement.

By the second week, he was confidently exploring the patio. By week three, he was sniffing dandelions in the backyard like an amateur botanist.

Emily's Realization: Leash Walks Aren't Walks

Not really. They're *sniff safaris*. Every trip outside was five feet forward, three feet back, and a solid thirty seconds spent staring at a leaf.

And that was okay. The point wasn't exercise—it was exploration.

Making the Carrier Less Scary

The carrier used to mean one thing: vet.

Emily wanted it to mean nap nook, snack bar, or at least "this isn't horrible."

Naturally, then, she left it out. She dropped treats in randomly. Sometimes she fed Miso *inside* it, just for fun. She even threw in one of his favorite blankets, the one that smelled like him.

Weeks passed. One day, she found Miso napping in it voluntarily.

Victory.

On the Road Again

Short drives were the next hurdle. Emily would buckle the carrier into the backseat, take a five-minute spin around the block, then come home and give Miso a treat.

The first time, he howled like an opera singer. The second time, less so. By the fifth, he sat quietly, looking out the mesh like a judgy little passenger.

When it came time for the next vet visit, no hiding. No wrestling. Just a wary look, a sigh, and a grudging climb into the carrier.

Progress.

Vet Prep: A Little Touch Goes a Long Way

Emily started handling Miso's paws gently during cuddle time. Sometimes she'd stroke his ears, peek in his mouth, rub his belly (only if he was in the mood).

During checkups, he didn't struggle. He still didn't *enjoy* it, but he cooperated. That was enough.

The Treat-Weighted Scale

One day, at the vet's office, Miso walked onto the scale all by himself.

Why? Because Emily had planted three of his favorite crunchy treats on it.

The vet blinked. "You trained your cat to weigh himself?"

Emily shrugged. "It seemed easier than wrestling."

Final Thoughts

These aren't just party tricks. Leash training, carrier calm, vet prep—these are gifts you give your future self. And your cat.

They say cats can't be trained.

But Emily trained Miso to explore grass, nap in a carrier, walk into a vet's office, and sit calmly on a scale.

Was it easy? Nope. Did it take time? Absolutely.

But for Miso, that training meant fewer terrifying moments. And for Emily, it meant fewer scratches, fewer guilt trips, and a lot more peace of mind.

Chapter 10: Your First 30 Days – A Simple Training Plan

Opening Story: "The Curious Case of the Couch Cat"

Exactly one month after bringing Miso home, Emily sat on the same couch he'd once tried to destroy with his claws and teeth and stared at the small purring lump curled beside her.

He used his litter box. He came (most of the time) when called. He knew "sit," and he played fetch with his favorite mouse.

He was still mischievous, still opinionated, still occasionally woke her up by knocking things off the nightstand—but now it felt less like chaos and more like...communication.

What had changed? Not Miso. *Emily* had changed—her expectations, her rhythm, and her ability to listen to her cat instead of lecturing him.

They hadn't "tamed" each other. They'd learned to speak the same language.

Why the First 30 Days Matter

These first few weeks aren't about mastering tricks or solving every problem. They're about laying groundwork: trust, routine, mutual understanding.

Emily didn't do everything right. She forgot playtime once and got ambushed at midnight. She fed Miso chicken once and discovered he was a diva about poultry forever after.

But she *showed up* day after day. And that mattered more than any checklist.

Still, a bit of structure helps. Here's the loose rhythm Emily followed, with plenty of grace for imperfection.

Week 1: Foundation & Familiarity

This week is about keeping things *simple*. Emily gave Miso one room to explore. Fed him at the same time each day. Left him alone when he needed space. Invited him in with gentle play.

By Day Three, he ventured out from his blanket fort. By Day Five, he was sleeping near her feet.

Trust doesn't arrive with a ribbon. It sneaks in when you're quiet, predictable, and kind.

Week 2: Introductions & Small Wins

Emily started clicker training with "come." It didn't go perfectly. One day, Miso sprinted over. The next, he stared at her like she was interrupting a very important nap.

Still, she repeated the cue. Offered the reward. Kept the tone light. Slowly, Miso began to connect the dots.

She also introduced a new scratching post and a second litter box. He eventually used both.

The lesson: *consistency over intensity*. One small success a day was enough.

Week 3: Problem Solving & Confidence Building

This was the week Miso jumped on the counter during a Zoom call and chewed through a charging cable.

Emily didn't freak out. (Okay, she *kind of* freaked out.)

Then she redirected him to his cat tree. Gave him a puzzle toy. Rewarded calm behavior.

That was the week "off" started to stick. The week Miso willingly walked into his carrier after a snack. The week Emily realized that most "bad behavior" was just unspent energy looking for an outlet.

Week 4: Connection & Celebration

By now, they had a groove. Miso came when called. Sat for treats. Greeted Emily at the door. Even tolerated the harness.

She started brushing his fur every night, not because it was part of a training plan, but because he leaned into it with that sleepy, slow-blink face.

Training had shifted from an activity to a relationship.

And the best part? Emily wasn't guessing anymore. She knew what his tail flick meant. She noticed when his play got too wild. She saw the shift from being overstimulated to content and could act accordingly.

Emily's Final Reflection

"I thought I was teaching Miso; she told a friend. But really, he was teaching me. How to slow down. How to listen. How to celebrate small things."

And maybe, most importantly, how to laugh when the cat knocks over your coffee *again*.

Closing Thoughts

There is no perfect plan. No magic formula.

But if you feed your cat on time, make room for play, and pay attention with kindness and curiosity, things will get easier. More connected. More fun.

By the end of thirty days, Emily didn't have a perfectly trained cat.

She had a companion.

www.ingramcontent.com/pod-product-compliance
Lightning Source LLC
LaVergne TN
LVHW020101090426
835510LV00040B/2761